Chapter 1

I am the visible person (TVP). You are TVP. She is TVP. He is TVP. We are TVP. They are TVP.

I experience a connection to you, her, him, us and them.

I experience these connections as though the connections have always existed and I just need to find them.

I feel completely dependent upon connection to others. I want connection. I need connection. When I find a connection and lose that connection, I feel as though my life will cease without that connection.

I depend upon my five senses to detect connection.

My connection to my body is a vast network of connection.

Within, I have tremendous awareness of a vast network of connection within. The hair on my arms provides incredible connection detection for me between the world outside of my body and within my body. My touch by my skin provides incredible connection detection for me with such a vast number of variations, my attempt to describe such vastness seems impossible for me.

I experience connection to pain and pleasure.

I experience connection to sight and sound.

I experience connection to smell and taste.

I experience connections to blood coursing through my body and my heart beating.

I experience my words as my words depart from my lips. Before my words depart from me, I sense my words within me and I sense my connection with my words.

I experience connection to my thoughts.

I learn about the vast number of connections between cells in my body, micro organisms inside and outside my body, communication between my cells, travel by my cells, intelligence and networking connections between my cells in my body, nerve connections, structural connections, mind-body connections, dream connections, respiration and ventilation connections, nutritional connections, vitality connections, hormone connections, functional connections, and more. I experience connections for all of these.

I experience connections when I interact with the world around me.

All of these connections... All around me, within me.... So many opportunities for connection experience.... So indescribable... So vast...

Chapter 2

Connection is important to me.

I love to immerse myself into my connection experiences. I love to discover new experiences of connection. I am able to get lost in my immersion experiences.

Chapter 3

When I have lost myself within my own connection immersion experience and returned, I am relieved to be back.

I have experienced an immersion experience of connections and attempted to return. I can only describe this experience as sheer panic. I call this experience "lost" as though I lost a connection so critical, so vital, so important, that unless I return, I shall cease to exist!

Chapter 4

My experience of connection is a vast potential all around me and within me.

When I witness a connection experience, I am able to record as a memory. I appreciate my memories of my connection experiences immensely.

I seem to retain a vast number of memories of connection experiences. When I search my memories, I am able to discover new connection experiences from my memories that I either did not realize I experienced prior to recording the memory, or perhaps I am able to record a memory which includes more connections than I experience. I enjoy this idea immensely. To be able to merely search my memories and discover more connection experiences is wonderful.

I have learned to explore my memories of connection experiences to discover connections. I am unable to detect a difference between my memory of a connection experience and a new connection experience "not from memory". I enjoy this idea that connection experience memories are just as real for me as new connection experiences for me.

I have learned to imagine connection experiences. I am unable to detect a difference between my imagined connection experience, my memory of connection experience and a new connection experience. I enjoy this idea that imagination is available to create new connection experiences and create memories of those new connection experiences.

Chapter 5

I have examined Nature to discover connections.

As I discover connections in Nature, I create memories of those connections. My connection experience memories provide my witness, my account, my observation as fact which I am able to share.

In school, my observations are considered valuable to others. I share my observations, my accounts, my witnessed connection experiences with others and they have evaluated my memories with letter grades. My teachers have compared my ability to recall my connection experience memories with other students. I suppose each of my teachers experience connections with some students comparatively different among their students. I am unable to detect my teacher's comparative connection experiences among his/her students, but my teacher describes the comparisons to be important and valuable. I accept my teacher's description, my teacher's story, my teacher's declaration that a comparison "exists" and the comparison is important and that I should imagine for myself the connection comparison is an experience for me so I will create a challenge within myself, a competition between myself and the other students. The challenge is to subject myself to my teacher's approval by various memory recall of connection experiences I have had presented in written, spoken and gesture. I can keep my challenge within myself alone, to provide my best attempts without any attempt to convince my teacher's assessment of me, to compete independently. Or, I can seek to demonstrate my connection experience memory recall directly to my teacher for special consideration and approval. Or, I can appeal to my teacher directly for approval instead and completely depart from the challenge my teacher presented in the first place. My teacher may allow me to appeal directly to him/her or my teacher may remind me of the "rules of the comparative competition" created by the

teacher for me to follow. I am only subject to my teacher's rules if I decide to be. I am clearly capable to act upon my own, to accept my teacher's game, create my own game, obey my teacher's rules, create my own rules, play the game, accept the challenge, reject the challenge or ignore all of the rules entirely and choose not to participate.

Chapter 6

In my family and in school, connections have been described to me about connection between myself and others. My family, my school teachers and my peers have evaluated these connections between myself and others and shared their conclusions with me. When I learn about these conclusions, I first learn about the connections they describe and I am able to experience the connection and record a memory of the connection experience.

My family and my teachers have categorized these connection experiences. There are many categories.

Connections between myself and others are first described to me. I learn about these connections and I experience them and record memories of my connection experiences, connections which family and teachers have described to me to exist. I accept the connection exists and I experience the connection and I record a memory of the experience.

My family and teachers describe comparisons between these connections. The comparisons of connections are given greater and lesser value by description. I accept the categories and the descriptions for each connection for the purpose of evaluation.

My family and teachers create a challenge for me to participate in, a game of uncountable rules to follow. The rules of the game include connection discovery, connection categorization, connection importance or value. The objective of the game is to have connection experiences in accordance with the rules of the game and avoid having connection experiences in accordance with the rules of the game. Compliance with the rules of the game is considered "good behavior". Non-compliance with the rules of the game is considered "bad behavior".

Every connection experience I have between myself and others is subject to this challenge, this set of rules within me, this set of rules about connections experienced: outside of myself; within myself, from memory recall and from imagination. Every connection experience is subject to the challenge, the game, the rules.

I accept my family's and my teacher's description, family's story and my teacher's story, my family's declaration and my teacher's declaration that these categories "exist", that comparison "exists", that categories are important with greater and lesser value descriptions, the comparisons of categories is important and that I should imagine for myself the category connection comparisons are experiences for me so I will create a challenge within myself, a competition between myself and myself. The challenge is to subject myself to my family's approval and my teacher's approval by various memory recall of connection experiences I have had presented in written, spoken and gesture. I can keep my challenge within myself alone, to provide my best attempts without any attempt to convince my family's assessment of me or my teacher's assessment of me, to compete independently. Or, I can seek to demonstrate my connection experience memory recall directly to my family or my teacher for special consideration and approval. Or, I can appeal to my family or my teacher directly for approval instead and completely depart from the challenge my teacher presented in the first place. My family or my teacher may allow me to appeal directly to him/her or my teacher may remind me of the "rules of the categories and comparative competition" created by my family and teacher for me to follow. I am only subject to my family's or my teacher's rules if I decide to be. I am clearly capable to act upon my own, to accept my family's game or my teacher's game, create my own game, obey my family's rules or my teacher's rules, create my own rules, play the game, accept the challenge, reject the challenge or ignore all of the rules entirely and choose not to participate.

Chapter 7

People described as "my peers" have described connections to me which I experienced and recorded to memory.

This category of people called "my peers" has a description I am unable to describe clearly, yet there are rules for the description of "my peers" which provide a means for me to categorize "included" and "excluded" in my "peer group".

I may subject myself to rules by "my peers", which are a challenge for me. I may participate independently in this challenge. I may appeal directly to a peer declared by the "peer group" as leader to improve my comparative value within the peer group. I may decide to create my own rules for the "peer group" and lead the group. I may decide to ignore the challenge entirely and choose to not participate in the "peer group" challenge designed with all of the rules for me to process in order to participate.

When I choose to participate in the "peer group" challenge, I must constantly compete with myself to follow the rules set by the leader of the "peer group" to ensure I am categorized by the leader of the "peer group" or by other leader-selected "peer group" members to remain within the "peer group".

While I challenge myself to remain within the "peer group", I discover the rules have potential to change dramatically. My new challenge is not merely to follow a set of rules. My challenge to follow the changing set of rules is also my challenge to remain within the "peer group".

My entire effort to participate in the "peer group" rules, the changing "peer group" rules, the exhausting categorization of my connection experiences, learning new connection experiences, recording new connection experience memories,

giving importance to every connection experience for evaluation purposes for maintaining acceptance by subjecting my connection experience observations communicated to my "peer group" by written, spoken and gesture: is exhaustive; is exhausting. My "peer group" leader or chosen delegates to consider my presented connection experience stories are the entirety of presentable testimony for consideration by my "peer group" to declare "in" or "out".

My connection experience of "in" is completely subject to approval.

My connection experience of "out" is completely subject to approval.

I am unable to control my own situation. I am unable to control my own circumstance. I am unable to control my participation "in" or "out" of "peer group".

I am capable of not participating.

Chapter 8

Rules to follow.

Connections to experience.

I accept challenges for myself to follow rules about connection experiences.

Why?

I believe I am not alone when I have connection experiences.

Chapter 9

When I married, I testified to the existence of my connection to my wife-to-be and I testified that I experienced that connection.

The government representative authorized to witness my testimony did not experience existence of my connection.

The government representative authorized to witness my testimony did not experience the connection I experienced.

The government representative authorized did witness my testimony and record of my testimony is the entire description for the role of the government representative.

The witness by the authorized government representative was not about my testimony, as though my description of my connection experienced was somehow valuable to this this authorized government representative. The entire purpose of witness was my declaration that I did observe a connection experience as fact and that I declared my own witness of my own experience, my belief that I did have a connection experience, that I did witness my own experience of a connection and that the connection experience I did have is of a connection which I believe firmly existed and continues to exist.

I made declaration of confirmed-witnessed-experienced-connection experience. I made "declaration testimony", I declared my own story about my own experience in an acceptable manner before the authorized government representative, who evaluated my testimony as acceptable or not acceptable, who evaluated my testimony as valuable for government purpose of recordation of "declared testimony" about my confirmed-witnessed-experienced-connection.

Chapter 10

During my marriage, I have given great value to the connection experience between myself and my wife.

Within a year, authorized representatives of "The Law" did witness my declaration of my connection experience with my adoptive son. As my son was considered by "The Law" to lack capacity for similar declaration, authorized representatives of "The Law" did consider the following evidence:
- Biological father did deny connection (relinquish)
- I did declare connection (adopt)
- Biological mother did declare connection (adopt OK)

Within a year, the witnessed declared connection was approved by "The Law". I had already declared my connection and considered the formal "approval by The Law" as redundant, however, I did celebrate the formal adoption. Connection experience of "family" is a marvelous experience of connection.

Chapter 11

During our marriage, my wife and I were able to declare a connection experience with a new born son. Our joy was not the declaration. Our joy was the connection experience.

Somehow, our connection experience with our son was also a new connection experience between us as parents. The abundance of connection experiences did not begin on the day of our son's birth though.

Before the birth of our first son together, I spoke to my son within my wife's womb. My son performed some rather amazing responses to my voice such as physically turning to the location of my voice seemingly to get his ear closer to the sound of my voice. Sometimes my son extruded himself rather far reaching beyond the boundary of his womb confines as much as three inches, possibly more.

My interactions with my son prior to his birth included an unintended outcome. After my son had positioned himself in "head out" direction for delivery, I played music for him higher on my wife's abdomen and he naturally adjusted himself toward the audio to listen more closely. Oops!

Fortunately, my mistake was masked later by physician's direction to perform a caesarean section.

I am well aware that a masked mistake is not a forgotten mistake.

Chapter 12

I find no failure, no mistake, no unintended outcome by NOT participating in these "expected experience challenges" presented to me by the numerous "groups" presenting the challenges. I find no understandable cause for any "group" to impose their challenge(s) upon me.

Their challenges, for me, are undeniably ABOUT my own experiences.